The Christian Handbook of Alphabetical Praise

Elevate Your Praise To God

Charles McCampbell, Sr.

Trilogy Christian Publishers
A Wholly Owned Subsidiary of Trinity Broadcasting Network
2442 Michelle Drive | Tustin, CA 92780
Copyright © 2024 by Charles McCampbell, Sr.

Scripture quotations marked NASB are taken from the New American Standard Bible® (NASB), Copyright © 1960, 1962, 1963, 1968, 1971, 1972, 1973, 1975, 1977, 1995 by The Lockman Foundation. Used by permission. www.Lockman.org. Scripture quotations marked NKJV are taken from the New King James Version®. Copyright © 1982 by Thomas Nelson. Used by permission. All rights reserved. Scripture quotations marked ESV are taken from the ESV® Bible (The Holy Bible, English Standard Version®), copyright © 2001 by Crossway Bibles, a publishing ministry of Good News Publishers. Used by permission. All rights reserved. Scripture quotations marked KJV are taken from the King James Version of the Bible. Public domain.

All rights reserved, including the right to reproduce this book or portions thereof in any form whatsoever.
For information, address Trilogy Christian Publishing
Rights Department, 2442 Michelle Drive, Tustin, CA 92780.
Trilogy Christian Publishing/ TBN and colophon are trademarks of Trinity Broadcasting Network.
For information about special discounts for bulk purchases, please contact Trilogy Christian Publishing.

Trilogy Disclaimer: The views and content expressed in this book are those of the author and may not necessarily reflect the views and doctrine of Trilogy Christian Publishing or the Trinity Broadcasting Network.

10 9 8 7 6 5 4 3 2 1
Library of Congress Cataloging-in-Publication Data is available.
ISBN 979-8-89333-213-1 | ISBN 979-8-89333-214-8 (ebook)

Table of Contents

Acknowledgements..............................5
Dedication....................................7
Introduction..................................9
Check This Out...............................13
Words Used for Loving on and Praising Our God:
    A...17
    B...19
    C...21
    D...23
    E...25
    F...27
    G...29
    H...31
    I...33
    J...35
    K...37
    L...39
    M...41
    N...43
    O...45
    P...47
    Q...49
    R...51

The Christian Handbook of Alphabetical Praise

S. 53
T. 55
U 57
V 59
W. 61
X 63
Y 65
Z. 67
Morning Prayer of Praise 69
Conclusion 71

Acknowledgements

I have had the joy of leading a wonderful group of people in worship. It's been my joy to not only be a worship leader, but a lead worshipper. That means freely expressing my love and admiration for our Lord and Savior Jesus Christ collectively with a strong body of believers. I received my introduction to corporate worship and praise at the Brooklyn Tabernacle Church. I also thank God for allowing me to serve in New York City as a member of the music group Soul Liberation, who made up the Creative Arts Division of Tom Skinner Associates. After moving to Dallas, TX, I became a member of the worship team at Oak Cliff Bible Fellowship. I am forever grateful for my family, my wife Deborah and our musically talented children. Nothing inspires me more than seeing a body of believers lifting their hands, their hearts, and their voices in praise to King Jesus. As a result of these experiences and these special groups of worshippers, I was moved and motivated to write *The Christian Handbook of Alphabetical Praise*! I hope this handbook will encourage you to spend less time reading, and more time loving on the King of kings and Lord of lords! Bless His holy name!

Dedication

This book is dedicated to my three brothers, Kelvin, Ray, and Derrick McCampbell, and to our wonderful mom and dad, who are with the Lord.

Introduction

THE CHRISTIAN HANDBOOK OF ALPHABETICAL PRAISE

Through the eyes of faith and the depth of living, I have concluded that God loves me in spite of myself. I believe that His lovingkindness is everlasting, His grace is sufficient, and His mercy endures forever. I believe that He has begun a good work in me that He indeed will complete. Therefore, my trust is completely in Him only. I give Him the praise when I am at my best, or when I am at my worst. I choose to not let my condition condition my worshipping and giving praise to the King of kings and Lord of lords. I thank and praise my God because He is immutable. That means that He does not change the way that people do. He is the same yesterday, today, and forevermore! Bless His holy name! If you don't feel as close to God as you used to be, guess who changed? Not God, but you. I was inspired to write *The Christian Handbook of Alphabetical Praise* out of a need and a desire in me to love on God and to offer Him the praise that He so deserves, every morning that He blesses me to open my eyes and see a brand-new day. My prayer is that this short handbook will move you to do the same—love on God every morning just because of who He is, and maintain a praying spirit throughout the day. I believe this will have a tremendous impact on your attitude and thoughts about God, yourself, and others. I am forever grateful to my beautiful family and friends who have helped me to grow stronger in my faith walk. I am especially thankful to God for His Word. David said in Psalm 119:105 (NASB), "Your word is a lamp to my feet and a light to my path." If there was ever a man in the Bible who knew how to praise God, it was David. It was David who said in Psalm 34:1 (NASB), "I will bless the Lord at all times; His praise shall continually be in my mouth." It was David who said in Psalm 103:1 (NASB), "Bless the Lord, O my soul, and all that is within me, bless His holy name." It was David who said in the very last Psalm (Psalm 150:1-2 NASB), "Praise the Lord! Praise God in His sanctuary; praise Him in His mighty expanse. Praise Him for His mighty deeds; praise Him according to His excellent greatness." He encourages the musicians to praise Him on their instruments in the sanctuary. He then concludes Psalm 150 by saying in v. 6 (NKJV), "Let everything that has breath praise the Lord. Praise the Lord!" Just remember that if you want God's presence, then offer Him praise, whether you are alone or with a group. God inhabits the praises of His people! So, I again encourage you to start your day off every morning

Introduction

by giving God the praise and thanksgiving for a brand-new day that you have never seen before. Hallelujah to our risen Savior and soon-coming King! King Jesus, the Messiah (Yeshua Hamashiak).

Check This Out

All through the Bible, men and women offered praise and worship to God in their different circumstances. These people understood that there is power in worshipping and praising God. For the believer, this provides not only an attitude check, but a heart check as well. As believers, we need to learn the value of praising and loving on God through our circumstances. That's how we claim victory over our circumstances and walk by faith every day. Although there are so many examples of men and women of faith in the Bible who praised God through their circumstances, I have selected seven of my favorites to use in this book.

(1) Exodus 15:20 (NKJV), "Then Miriam the prophetess, the sister of Aaron, took the timbrel in her hand; and all the women went out after her with timbrels and with dances. And Miriam answered them: 'Sing to the Lord, for He has triumphed gloriously! The horse and its rider He has thrown into the sea.'" This was right after God delivered them from Pharoah's army.

(2) Exodus 15:1-2 (NKJV), "Then Moses and the children of Israel sang this song to the Lord, and spoke, saying: 'I will sing to the Lord, for He has triumphed gloriously! The horse and its rider He has thrown into the sea!

The Lord is my strength and song, and He has become my salvation; He is my God, and I will praise Him; my father's God, and I will exalt Him.'" Moses (like Miriam), along with the children of Israel, was praising God for delivering them from Pharoah's army.

(3) 1 Chronicles 29:10-13 (NKJV), "Therefore David blessed the Lord before all the assembly; and David said: 'Blessed are You, Lord God of Israel, our Father, forever and ever. Yours, O Lord, is the greatness, the power and the glory, the victory and the majesty; for all that is in heaven and in earth is Yours; Yours is the kingdom, O Lord, and You are exalted as head over all. Both riches and honor come from You, and You reign over all. In Your hand is power and might; in Your hand it is to make great and to give strength to all. Now therefore, our God, we thank You and praise Your glorious name.'" David was praising God for how the people had rejoiced and offered so willingly.

(4) Nehemiah 8:6 (NKJV), "And Ezra blessed the Lord, the great God. Then all the people answered, 'Amen, Amen!' while lifting up their hands. And they bowed their heads and worshiped the Lord with their faces to the ground." All Ezra did was read the Law of Moses to the people. Then praise erupted! Hallelujah!

(5) Luke 2:20 (NKJV), "Then the shepherds returned,

glorifying and praising God for all the things that they had heard and seen, as it was told them." The shepherds were fired up about seeing the Christ child.

(6) Acts 16:25 (NASB), "But about midnight Paul and Silas were praying and singing hymns of praise to God, and the prisoners were listening to them."

(7) 2 Chronicles 20:22 (NKJV), "Now when they began to sing and to praise, the Lord set ambushes against the people of Ammon, Moab, and Mount Seir, who had come against Judah; and they were defeated." Read the story of Jehoshaphat in 2 Chronicles 20:1-30 and behold the power of God through praise!

WORDS USED FOR LOVING ON AND PRAISING OUR GOD

Alpha – The beginning

Almighty – There is none more powerful

Anointed King – Christ, the **Anointed** One

Advocate – The one who intercedes on our behalf

Anchor – Our mainstay and stability

Author and Finisher of Our Faith – The one on whom we stake our eternal destiny

WORDS USED FOR LOVING ON AND PRAISING OUR GOD

Bright and Morning Star – Jesus, the Christ

Beginning – The Originator and Creator

Beloved Savior – He who is loved and adored by all who know that He is the Christ

Bread of Life – The living Word

Bridegroom – Refers to the way Christ gave Himself on the cross and the way a husband and wife give themselves to one another

WORDS USED FOR LOVING ON AND PRAISING OUR GOD

The *Christ* – Jesus

Chief Cornerstone – Jesus is the foundation of our salvation

Wonderful *Counselor* – One of the names that the Christ child was referred to as, even at His birth

Creator – God **created** everything that exists

WORDS USED FOR LOVING ON AND PRAISING OUR GOD

Deliverer – One who came to free His people from sin

Dayspring – Sunrise from on high to bring light to all men

Door Opener – Jehovah Jireh, the one who provides and opens **doors** that no man can shut

Doorway to Heaven – Jesus is the only way to heaven (John 14:6)

WORDS USED FOR LOVING ON AND PRAISING OUR GOD

Eternal God – He is the great God of omnipresence

Everlasting Father – He has no beginning or end

The *End* – Omega; there is no God besides Me

Elohim – Supreme or mighty one

WORDS USED FOR LOVING ON AND PRAISING OUR GOD

Faithful – The one on whom we can depend

Father – Our heavenly **Father,** who watches over us

Friend – Jesus, the one who laid down His life for us

WORDS USED FOR LOVING ON AND PRAISING OUR GOD

God Almighty – Great **God** of omnipotence

Glorious King – He who is worthy of all **glory**

Good Shepherd – One who laid down His life for His sheep

Giver of New Life – In Christ, we have new life

WORDS USED FOR LOVING ON AND PRAISING OUR GOD

Heavenly Father – Our Father, who is in **heaven**

High Priest – The one who gave His life as an atonement for the sins of the world

Holy One – He who came down from heaven and is without sin

Head of the Church – Christ, the **head** of the church

Ha Mashiach – Messiah in Hebrew

WORDS USED FOR LOVING ON AND PRAISING OUR GOD

Immanuel – God is with us

I Am – The existing One

Indwelling Spirit – The Holy Spirit of God who **indwells** all believers

Image of the Invisible God – The Son, Jesus, is the **image** of the **invisible** God

WORDS USED FOR LOVING ON AND PRAISING OUR GOD

Jesus – The Son of God

Jehovah Jireh – Our Provider

Jehovah Nissi – The Lord is Conqueror

Judge – Jesus is the righteous **Judge**

K

WORDS USED FOR LOVING ON AND PRAISING OUR GOD

King of Glory – All glory belongs to Him

King of Kings – Above Him, there is no other

King of the Jews – Jesus is the real **King** of the Jews, both at the beginning and end of His life

L

WORDS USED FOR LOVING ON AND PRAISING OUR GOD

Lamb of God – Jesus, who takes away the sin of the world

The *Life* – Jesus said, "I am the way, the truth, and the **life**. No one comes to the Father except through me" (John 14:6 NKJV)

Love – God is **love** (1 John 4)

Lord of Lords – He reigns supreme

Lover of My Soul – Jesus has unchanging and unconditional **love** for us

Light of the World – Jesus is the **Light** of the world. In Him there is no darkness

Living Word – "Thy word is a lamp unto my feet, and a light unto my path" (Psalm 119:105 KJV)

M

WORDS USED FOR LOVING ON AND PRAISING OUR GOD

Messiah – Jesus, who suffered because of the sins of others

Master – The one to whom we surrender our lives as Lord

Mediator – The one who took God by one hand and man by the other and brought us together

Most High God – El Elyon, the God who fulfills His purpose for us

Miracle Worker – The God who makes the impossible possible

N

WORDS USED FOR LOVING ON AND PRAISING OUR GOD

New Life Giver – He has provided for us a right to the tree of life by His Spirit

Jesus of *Nazareth* – The Savior of the world and the incarnation of God

WORDS USED FOR LOVING ON AND PRAISING OUR GOD

Omega – The first and the beginning

God of *Omnipresence* – Everywhere at the same time in the past, present, and future

God of *Omnipotence* – All powerful, almighty

God of *Omniscience* – All knowing, all wise

The *One* True God – God the Father, God the Son, and God the Holy Spirit, the Triune God

WORDS USED FOR LOVING ON AND PRAISING OUR GOD

Prince of Peace – Jesus, Yeshua

Precious Lord – Our Lord and Savior, Jesus Christ

Prophet – The one chosen by God

Powerful Savior – He who has the **power** to save the lost

WORDS USED FOR LOVING ON AND PRAISING OUR GOD

Quintessential – You are more than **quintessential**; You are more than the ultimate

Quickly – The God who moves **quickly** on behalf of His people

Quiet – He leads me beside the **quiet** waters

R

WORDS USED FOR LOVING ON AND PRAISING OUR GOD

Righteous King – The King of kings and **righteous** Judge

Redeemer – Christ, who gave His life for our redemption

Rock – Jesus, our **Rock** and Deliverer

S

WORDS USED FOR LOVING ON AND PRAISING OUR GOD

Sovereign God – Ruler with absolute power

Savior of the World – Gave His life because of His amazing love for mankind

Sar Shalom – Hebrew for Prince of Peace

Son of God – Jesus

Son of Man – Jesus

Servant – One who ministers

T

WORDS USED FOR LOVING ON AND PRAISING OUR GOD

Trustworthy Lord – One you can depend on

The Way, the *Truth*, and the Life – Jesus

Teacher – One who gives instructions to the wise

U

WORDS USED FOR LOVING ON AND PRAISING OUR GOD

Understanding God – He knows and **understands** every thing that we are faced with in life

Uplifter of My Head – "You, O Lord, are a shield about me, my glory, and the lifter of my head" (Psalm 3:3 ESV)

Upholder – You sustain

WORDS USED FOR LOVING ON AND PRAISING OUR GOD

God of *Veracity* – You are the God of truth. All truth

   is Yours

God of *Victory* – In You we have the **victory**

WORDS USED FOR LOVING ON AND PRAISING OUR GOD

All-*Wise* God – All-knowing God. Great God of omniscience

Wonderful Savior – Jesus, You gave Your life to save the lost

Worthy – So deserving of all our praise and worship. You are great and greatly to be praised

WORDS USED FOR LOVING ON AND PRAISING OUR GOD

Xerox – Lord, make my life like a **Xerox** copy of Your love, so that men would see my good works and give glory to my Father in heaven

X-ray – Lord, Your ability to see into my heart is greater than **x-ray** vision

WORDS USED FOR LOVING ON AND PRAISING OUR GOD

Yahweh – The name for the God of the Israelites.

>**Yahweh** is salvation

Yeshua – The Hebrew name for Jesus

You – Lord, **You** are the same **yesterday,** today, and forevermore

Z

WORDS USED FOR LOVING ON AND PRAISING OUR GOD

Zeal – Thank You for giving me the **zeal** to share my faith and win souls for the kingdom

Zenith – High point

Great God from *Zion* – A hill in Jerusalem on which the temple was built

HERE'S MY MORNING PRAYER OF PRAISE:

(EXAMPLE)

Dear Lord, I thank You for opening my eyes to see a brand-new day. I confess that this is the day that the Lord has made, so I will rejoice and be glad in it. I praise You, Lord, today, according to Your excellent greatness; I praise You according to Your mighty deeds; I praise You for how awesome You are. Let everything that has breath praise the Lord. Praise the Lord!

Dear God, I praise You because You are **ALPHA, ALMIGHTY**. You are our **ADVOCATE, BREAD** of LIFE, **BEGINNING, BELOVED** SAVIOR, **CHRIST, CHIEF CORNERSTONE, DELIVERER, DAYSPRING**. Oh God, You are **ELOHIM, ETERNAL** GOD, **EVERLASTING FATHER, FRIEND,** so **FAITHFUL** is Your name. Lord, You are **GOD** Almighty, **GOOD** Shepherd, **GLORIOUS** King. My **God,** You are my **HEAVENLY** Father, **HIGH** Priest, **HAMASHIAK, INDWELLING** Spirit, the Great **I Am I that I Am**, **JESUS, JEHOVAH JIREH, KING of KINGS, LORD of LORDS, LAMB** of God, **LIVING** Word, **MASTER, MIGHTY** God, **MESSIAH.** Thank You, Lord, for being our **MEDIA-**

TOR, Jesus of **NAZARETH,** our giver of **NEW** Life, our Great God of **OMNISCIENCE, OMNIPRESENCE**, and **OMNIPOTENCE, POWERFUL** Savior, **PRINCE of PEACE**. Lord, You move **QUICKLY** on behalf of Your people, You are our **RIGHTEOUS REDEEMER** and our **ROCK, SOVERIGN SAVIOR** of the world. Lord, You are **SAR SHALOM** (Price of Peace), **TRUSTWORTHY** Lord and **TEACHER**. You are the **UPLIFTER** of our heads who **UNDERSTANDS** all things. You are the God of **VERACITY** who gives us **VICTORY** day by day. Oh Lord, You are our **WONDERFUL** Savior and all-**WISE** God. Lord, make my life as clear as a **XEROX** copy of Your love, that men would see my good works and give glory to Your name. I say **YES** to Your will, for You are **YESHUA, YAHWEH,** and the **ZENITH** (High Point) of my life. I give You praise, oh great God from **ZION**.

CONCLUSION:

Now take the amazing English alphabet and create your own daily prayer of praise to our heavenly Father, and watch the impact that it will have on your walk with the Lord. Share this with your family and friends in the faith. Let voices of praise and worship resound from all over the earth. God is worthy of all praise, glory, and honor! Let everything that has breath praise the Lord!

PRAISE THE LORD!

Milton Keynes UK
Ingram Content Group UK Ltd.
UKHW020810080824
446708UK00026BA/319